# Reiki Retreats

*Practical Guide*

**Justine Melton**

# Copyright

© 2018, Acorn Gecko SRL

ALL RIGHTS RESERVED. This book contains material protected under International and Federal Copyright Laws and Treaties. Any unauthorized reprint or use of this material is prohibited. No part of this book may be reproduced or transmitted in any form or by any means, electronic or mechanical, including photocopying, recording, or by any information storage and retrieval system without express written permission from the publisher.

# Table of Contents

Introduction ...................................................................5

Chapter 1: Benefits of Reiki Retreats ............................7

Chapter 2: How to Select the Right Location ..............11

Chapter 3: How to Select the Perfect Time ................21

Chapter 4: Marketing & How to Find Attendees .........27

Chapter 5: How to Plan a Retreat ...............................35

Chapter 6: Planning Your Retreat Budget ...................41

Chapter 7: Expected & Unexpected Issues When Planning a Retreat ......................................................51

Chapter 8: Sending Reiki to Your Retreat ...................59

Chapter 9: Sample Plan Blueprints .............................63

Chapter 10: Types of Retreats ....................................69

Chapter 11: The Main Topic of Your Retreat ..............73

Chapter 12: Self-love Reiki Retreat Blueprint .............79

Chapter 13: Items to Sell at a Reiki Retreat ................87

Chapter 14: Guest Speakers .......................................93

Chapter 15: Animal Partners ......................................97

Chapter 16: Protecting Yourself Before Group Exercises & Energy Exchange ..................................101

Chapter 17: Fun Group Exercises ............................107

Chapter 18: Reiki Take Home Gifts…Thank you! ........117
About the Author..............................................................123

# Introduction

Have you ever thought about doing a Reiki Retreat but thought that it took too much work to put together? Perhaps, you think that you have to have decades of experience in the Reiki field or be an all-knowing expert to share your knowledge with others? With a little planning and creativity anyone in the Reiki field can have a retreat! Each of us is different and has so many unique perspectives to share with our Reiki community. This book is a complete guide of how to plan a Reiki Retreat from start to finish that is truly your own. There are many examples, exercises and sample plans included every step of the way.

I have enjoyed putting all the fine details together to encourage as many people as possible to share their light with the world. Reiki Retreats are a gift of time to others that allow them to grow, explore and experiment with all that is Reiki. It is an amazing gift that can change someone's entire life.

I would like to thank my family for giving me the time to put this book together and of course, the patience and love of everyone at Reiki Rays.

It is my hope that you will use this book as a blueprint for your own Reiki Retreat and then fearlessly make it your own. Please share any of the ideas that you love in this book with others. You never know who you might inspire or what small thing can cause a positive breakthrough in a person's life.

Sending you love,
Justine Melton
RMT, Intuitive Counselor, Psychic Medium

# Chapter 1: Benefits of Reiki Retreats

Reiki Retreats are a special gift of time that we can put together to help spread light through the Universe. Retreats offer the unique opportunity for people to take a step back, turn off the outside world, and allow themselves to become even greater beacons of light. Having a Reiki Session is a gift to ourselves. Attending a well-planned out and loving retreat is the equivalent of having a Reiki session that lasts for an entire weekend or more. It gives your soul the chance to rest, renew and grow and your mind a chance to soar.

Planning a Reiki retreat may seem a bit daunting at first or a big task that only a very experienced Reiki Master may complete. This is a huge misconception that I try hard to dispel. While it will take a great deal of commitment and some time on your part it can be done by a Reiki Practitioner of any level. Reiki Retreats are an endless gift that often goes unused. There are so many amazing benefits that they offer to both the organizer as well as to the participant. These benefits include but are not limited to…

- Gifting yourself time to expand
- Gifting yourself self-love
- Allowing yourself to turn off the outside world and go within
- New friendships & possibly even family
- Networking
- Being with likeminded people
- Being a part of a group
- A sense of community
- Learning to use your gifts in a new way
- Peace
- Feeling the power of group energy

- Realizing how important your role can be in a group setting
- Support
- Guidance
- Love
- A feeling of accomplishment
- The excitement of having new things to share with the world after you have completed the retreat
- The sparking of new ideas within yourself
- Being able to encourage others to use their gifts
- Feeling more power within
- Being able to have a stronger connection with Reiki energy
- Feeling a higher vibrational level
- Opening the door to a magical world of natural self-healing
- Realizing your own power
- Making new discoveries about the mind, body, soul connection

If a retreat is planned carefully and filled with love, it can truly offer life changing energy for all involved. Feel your power, gather up some courage and allow yourself to explore the area of creating a retreat. If you allow love and all of the Reiki Retreat benefits to flow into your planning then, Reiki will be sure to expand and nourish each soul during your retreat. Creating a new Reiki Retreat is an awesome and limitless gift you can give to yourself and others. How cool is that?!

# Chapter 2: How to Select the Right Location

Picking the right Reiki location can really make or break your retreat. It is one of the most important decisions you will make while creating your retreat. Do you want to be close to nature? Do you want to have the retreat be more business like and in an office building? Do you want to have it in a church that matches your own religion? Do you want it to appeal to older people, younger, or a mix of both? Is the retreat for families? Are you looking for a spot where there can be a lot of group work or is there mainly going to be guest speakers? If it is outdoors what will the weather be like? Do you need to plan around certain seasons? The questions you need to ask yourself may seem a bit overwhelming at first but let's take a minute and simplify everything.

Go with your first thought! Don't doubt it. It doesn't have to be exact. This first thought just shows you where your deepest interest might be. You have plenty of time to experiment with a few different options or to even change your mind! You may have a few different ideas and that is ok! Pick one idea to think about at a time and we can go over what might be best for each idea below. Let's make picking the location an easy next step!

**Retreat locations possibilities:**

- *At your home or the home of a friend*

This sort of retreat is usually on a smaller scale and can be great to help build your confidence with being able to host a meaningful retreat. You will most likely feel safe and secure in your home or that of your friends. The more comfortable you feel during your retreat will help you to create the most laid back environment possible. Having people feel comfortable is one of the best things you can do to create a space where they can focus on themselves and expand to new areas. If you feel insecure or uptight, the energy in the room will be bad and people will find it harder to relax and be a part of the group. Having it at home can also save you a lot of money. You will not have to pay to rent a space and you will already have things such as a kitchen and bathroom in your space. Little things such as décor, heat/air conditioning, music players, candles, seating can all add up fast. Most of this you will already have at home and will probably only need to buy a few more things. Participants may stay in your home for a fee or stay at a hotel close by if the retreat is more than a day. Home retreats can be a great starting place to run through everything before you take it to a bigger scale.

- *Office Space/Hotel Conference Center*

Having a retreat at an office space or at a hotel conference center can make your retreat seem more professional. However, you really need to think about where your type pf retreat fits in. Is it something that would be more effective in a Conference center or is it something that would do better in the outdoors? Do you need to be in a more homely and comforting space or will your topic be able to be presented better in a large public space? When you choose to have it in an office space or a conference center, you do not have to worry about having strangers in your home. While everyone has the best intention when planning for a retreat, you need to keep your own personal safety in mind. Obviously, having strangers in your home does not always pose a threat. However, you do need to be aware of safety issues. Hotels and conference centers may be able to provide food, lodging and other incentives for you all in one spot. They may also offer you package deals. However, this can be very costly and often times you have to pay a large deposit or all of it upfront before you even have your retreat. A huge benefit to having it in a public location like this is that you are able to have a larger amount of people attend. You also only have to think about the actual retreat material that you will be presenting and do not have to worry about your home being a sort of bed and breakfast environment or having to entertain people for several days. Make sure to be aware that depending on what exercises you have planned, insurance issues may come into play. Check with the location first to make sure you are covered for anything that you want to do. That will give you time to secure the proper insurance if you or they do not already have it. A good example of this would be needing insurance at the property location when having an equine Reiki retreat.

- **Outdoor Nature Retreat**

    The mountains, desert, and coastal beaches offer a wide array of possibilities. It is so easy to plan an extended retreat at any of these locations because of the natural surroundings that are offered. Sometimes there are vacation rentals that you can rent out or even spaces where they rent spots for special retreats. Campgrounds are another option at the right time of the year. You can usually get a really good discounted rate on campsites or little one room cabins. There are usually public meetings spaces at these locations included as well. Some even have little outdoor fireplaces, streams, lakes, trails, pools, food stands, etc. The possibilities are endless. If you choose to have your retreat somewhere like this, you should be sure to send your participants lists of what items they need to bring with them to be comfortable at your outdoor location. Also, let them know if you will be providing food and if you are not a list of where they may purchase food and average prices is always helpful. You may even talk to a few businesses in the area ahead of time and agree to recommend that your retreat members frequent their business is they offer them a special discount on purchases. You also will need to usually pay ahead of time and sometimes may need to get a permit for certain public spaces. This is usually relatively easy to do. Also, the nature sounds and natural wonders offer a lot of extras that you just won't find in a regular home or conference center.

When you know the type of location that you'd like to hold your retreat at think about ways you can make it more affordable. Do you have any friends that live or have vacation homes in that area? Do they have friends that do or know of any spots in the area that offer discounts? If so you may be able to work out a deal with them that makes it much more affordable for everyone. There are always deals out there. Once you know the general area of where you'd like to have it send some Reiki to it! It never hurts and you will be sure that your location is for the greatest good of all. Start investigating and have some fun while planning your retreat.

## Tips on How to Create the Perfect Reiki Space on a Budget

When you walk into your Reiki Space take a look around. What do you notice? Is it warm and inviting? Do you feel relaxed or do you feel anxious, unsure? It is important to note here that everyone has their own style and that is ok! However, **no matter what your style is a client should be able to walk in and feel at peace.**

**Top 5 Tips for Creating the Perfect Reiki Space on a Budget:**

• **Take everything out of the space!** Does this seem dramatic? It might but actually it allows you to truly have a blank space that things are slowly added back into. Not everything will make its way back into the office and that's ok!

- **The .99 cent store is your friend!** Here in The United States we have some stores where you can find a lot of stuff for just .99 cents. Also, discount stores are great and hand making somethings can offer huge savings.
- **Make a plan of what you want before you do it.** What are the things you can do to create the biggest difference? Would changing the paint color help? Adding more or less light?
- **Simple is your friend!** I like to go with as simple as possible no matter what your style is. Any style can be made simple. The less clutter there is in a room the more room there is to focus on healing and the more positive energy there will be.
- The few things I always put in a space: **White candles, plants, soft lighting and soft music.** If you are artistic you can even make your own artwork. Add in a Reiki table and a few extra chairs and you are all set. Really you do not need more! Less is more in healing spaces.

For budget only purposes, here are my recommendations:

- Clear Glass Vases (these can be used for plants or for candles)
- Fresh Flowers
- Live Plants
- Music
- Frames for Certificates and/or pictures
- Tables/Chairs/Lights
- Candles
- Reiki Certificates & Teaching Supplies

The space you practice Reiki in plays a big part in your clients' healing. If done correctly it can comfort them and allow them to be more open to receiving the healing.

The more open they are to the Reiki energy the better the Reiki energy can help them.

# Chapter 3: How to Select the Perfect Time

Retreats can happen at any time of the year. There really are no set rules that say you must have a certain type of retreat on a certain day of the year. There are however, different times of the year where you may have more success than others. Things like energy, holidays, and weather can have a huge influence on people wanting to attend. For example, if you are having a Reiki Self-love Retreat you may find that the most beneficial month of the year to have it is February. This is the month of love and people will have love of all forms on their mind. During this time people see love energy (manufactured and real) all around them and will be more likely to be seeking love out in others or themselves. It is a time of the year where people also may realize that their self-love is lacking and because of all the love energy everywhere may be more likely to sign up for your retreat.

There are several things to consider when deciding what time of the year would be best for your retreat. Let's take a look at what some of the most important factors are and the different times of the year you might have the most success with your specific retreat.

**January:** January is a great time of the year to have any retreat that deals with New Year's resolutions, rebirth of any kind, or learning something new for the New Year. Good retreats for this time of the year can be any that have to do with learning a new Reiki level, Reiki Year Prediction Retreat, How to Incorporate Reiki into new areas of your life Retreat, or Reiki Affirmations for a New Life Retreat.

**February-March:** This is the time of year to focus on love and self-care. Emotions can run high at this time. Retreats involving love, emotional connections and emotional healing can have great success. Examples of retreats that you can have at this time of the year would be a Reiki Your Way to Self-love Retreat, Reiki Emotional Release Retreat, and Reiki Soul Mate Retreat.

**April-May:** Spring is a great time to do spring cleaning in all areas of your life. The energy is perfect for cleaning house. It is also perfect for working with children. Great retreats for this time of the year would be a Reiki Hoarders Anonymous Retreat, Reiki Cleansing Retreat, Reiki Aura Clearing Retreat, and a Bringing Reiki to Children Retreat.

**June-July-August:** The summer is a more laid back time of the year that is great for any type of retreat having to do with creativity, music, animals, nature, and friendship. If you are in a part of the world where the seasons are opposite of those in The United States please simply match the months to your own season if you feel called to do so. Some awesome examples for this time of the year would be a Reiki & Sound Healing Retreat, Reiki Jewelry Retreat, Reiki Your Way to Likeminded Friendships Retreat, Animal Reiki or Reiki & Mother Nature Retreat. If you celebrate Earth Day you can also have success with the Reiki & Mother Nature Retreat in the spring as well.

**September-October:** This time of the year the energy is incredible for letting go of anything that does not serve you. It is also great for facing darkness, facing fears, clearing negative spirits, helping souls cross over, learning to communicate with your spirit guides and celebrating departed loved ones. The veil between worlds is the thinnest at this time of the year. Use this to your benefit! You are not only helping yourself but you are helping anyone else that attends your retreat as well. Examples of positive retreats for this time of the year are Reiki to Combat Darkness Retreat, Reiki to Allow Letting Go Retreat, Reiki Communication With Spirits Retreat, and Reiki Soul Connect Retreat.

**November-December:** Retreats at the end of the year offer amazing energy for introspection, release and fine tuning. Meditative work and intuition building is very powerful at this time of the year. You can also get a jump start at detoxing before the start of the New Year. Examples of retreats for this time of the year would be a Reiki Intuition Building Retreat, Reiki Meditation Power Retreat, and Reiki Detox Retreat.

While there are key times of the year that offer more power for specific types of retreats, there are also a few secondary factors that come into play. If you are a believer in the Astrology world you might want to pay attention to things like when Mercury goes into retrograde or what transits are happening that would make your retreat the most successful. Perhaps you like to closely follow the seasons and have noticed the different powers found around the different solstices. Maybe your vibration gets the most power from the Summer Solstice or perhaps your retreat would pair best with the Winter Solstice. Please don't forget these important energy sources when planning your retreat!

An important thing to keep in mind is the cycle of the moon. During full moons retreats that deal with release, clearing, cleansing and truths coming to light will be the most powerful. New moons on the other hand, can bring extra success to learning new things, setting intentions, going down new paths in life and manifesting abundance. Are there any special moons happening that might bring you extra healing powers that you are looking for? Take the time to research it and have the energetic flow on your side.

Thinking ahead and planning a retreat at the time of the year offering the best energy is worth it! When Reiki and The Universe have your back, your retreat can offer an amazing portal of positive healing energy. Plan ahead! You will not be disappointed.

# Chapter 4: Marketing & How to Find Attendees

You have learned how to build a fabulous retreat and are ready to go. Now, you just need people to sign up. How do you find the attendees? How do you advertise? Will people think your idea is as great as you do? Unfortunately, just putting a flyer up around town most likely will not get many people into your retreat. However, with planning and an understanding of the best ways to market your retreat it does not have to be hard. It will take some planning in the beginning but after a little work you should have a successful game plan that will get you known in the retreat world.

## Top Ways to Find Attendees:

- **Friend Run Through/Word of Mouth:** I always recommend doing a run through of your retreat with friends before doing your first official one. This way you can work out anything that doesn't flow correctly. Sometimes things can work good in theory but play out differently when you are actually experiencing it. The other benefit is that the retreat should build excitement with your friends. They will be forgiving and understanding of any kinks that you may need to work out. They should also be very honest with ways that you can improve! Honest feedback is an extremely useful thing to have before your retreat is open to the public. If they enjoyed your retreat they will recommend it to others. You can even offer a friends & family discount to get people to sign up for your first official retreat. The goal is to get people in the door the 1st time. After that, your attendees will recommend your retreat to others and you will start to build your retreat business. Word of mouth is extremely important and can bring in the most in person business for you.

- **Social Media:** Social Media is your friend! Make an ad and put it on Facebook and Instagram. Have a Twitter account? Do a tweet notifying your followers about an upcoming retreat and how cool it will be. Tweet out an incentive! Sometimes there is a small fee to put out ads on different social media platforms. It is worth every penny and I highly recommend it to get your retreat some attention. The ad can target specific audiences that you select and your online friends can share it with their friends. Once it is out there the possibilities are endless of where it can go. It can be liked and shared multiple times so countless people are able to see it. If an attendee is going to your retreat and is excited about it they can share your information with their own friends and get a group of their friends to attend together. The possibilities are endless here.

- **Website/Blog:** If you have a website or a blog you can post an ad for it there, post a special discount, send an info link out to your subscribers and make informational posts about it that generate excitement. You can also post pictures of cool objects that you might have at your retreat that can gain interest in it as well.

- **Client Discount:** If you have a Reiki business you can offer your clients a discount for your retreat. You can also offer a discount to them if they get a friend to sign up.

- **Pamphlets/Flyers:** You can make pamphlets and flyers and leave them at places people who would be interested in your retreat might frequent. For example, depending on the type of retreat this might be a counseling office, coffee/tea shop, dance studio, gym, yoga studio, spiritual business, natural grocery store, gem store, etc. If you do decide to make pamphlets or flyers pay attention to the types of artwork used. It should be something simple and striking that will pull someone in enough to get them to read about your retreat. Art has great power! Do not underestimate the power of good artwork.

- **Networking Magic:** Have friends that are counselors, teachers, doctors, stable owner, animal trainer or anyone that might want to recommend their clients attend your retreat? You can make a friendly deal with them that benefits both of you. If you are having a guest speaker at your retreat I highly recommend networking with them as well.

- **Friends & Family Discount:** Have a special discount for friends and family. Also, offer a special discount if they get other people to sign up.

- **Incentives:** Offer incentives in your retreat ad. For example, if you are doing a self-love retreat the first 10 people to sign up receive a Rose Quartz necklace. You can also offer an incentive for the person who has the most referrals sign up. The person with the most referrals can win something like a 5 session Reiki pass with you, a free retreat pass, or a self-love reading. It should be something related to the retreat that they will be excited about getting.

## *Tips on How to start a Reiki Community*

I'd like to share with you different ways that you can start a Reiki Community where you live. It really is so simple and can have lasting positive effects on you and the entire community.

- **Join Meetup.com** and see if there is any sort of Reiki community. If there is give it a shot and go to a meeting. If you don't find the group is for you start your own group on meetup with your own unique twist. Chances are someone is looking for the same thing as you.

- **Go to alternative and holistic book stores** and ask them if they offer any type of Reiki Sessions or if they have a Reiki Group. If they do offer something then get the contact information for the Reiki Master and contact them about Reiki get together in the community.
- **Google Reiki Masters in the city you are in.** See which ones you feel called too. Call or email them and ask any questions you have or ask if they are willing to meet up with you. I have never come across a Reiki Master that didn't want to talk to someone new in the area or offer advice for how to get a group together.
- After talking to some people offer to **host a Reiki night in your home**. If you enjoy your evening make any tweaks you might need to and turn it into a monthly event. Maybe different people in the group can sign up to take turns hosting it at your house. Have it be a potluck style so that the host is not always out money. Another idea is to just do coffee/tea and have everyone bring a homemade treat to share.
- Start **talking to people on alternative healing sites and blogs**.

- Put up flyers in your area advertising **a free Reiki meetup group.**
- Put up flyers in your area for **an alternative healing meetup group.** I have found this to be a lot of fun. Everyone can share their own healing styles, you can learn so much and can make lasting friendships with these like-minded people.

# Chapter 5: How to Plan a Retreat

You have now looked at all of the amazing benefits that Reiki Retreats offer, have an idea of what type of retreat you might want to have and where you would like to have it. Now it is time to learn how to plan it! Don't worry. It may seem overwhelming at first, but if we break it down into smaller areas you will have it planned in no time and all.... and without a headache. I promise!

Planning a Reiki Retreat is similar to planning a class. The only real difference is that it most likely will be longer than a traditional class and you have meals and lodging to consider. I like to tell people that Reiki Retreats can be thought of as a Reiki Meet. Acronyms can be fun and really help us break down the basics. The basic steps can be easily remembered this way!

**Reiki MEET=**

    **M: Meet & Greet / Hello!**

    **E: Engage/Lecture**

    **E: Exercises**

    **T: Talk**

Let's spend a minute looking at each section of a Reiki Meet a bit deeper now.

**M (Meet):** This is where you plan how you wish to have everyone meet and greet. This is the 1st impression of what your retreat will be like. Take the time to make sure it is welcoming and inclusive of everyone. Some things that you might want to consider are having name tags for everyone. Calling each other by name, having a spot to grab a glass of water or a cup of tea or coffee before sitting down can help break the ice and allow everyone to feel more comfortable. Also, if you have a few tables set up with sample items that you will be using during the retreat (such as, handouts, crystals, salt, candles, etc) it can really help make people feel comfortable, interested and excited about what they are going to experience that day.

Having a comfortable place for people to sit is key. I like to have everyone in front of me or in a crescent (half circle) shape. I love circles but I don't like talking with my back to anyone. One of my goals during a retreat is for everyone to feel that they are equally important. I also want everyone to have the chance to get the best experience possible out of our time together. If my back is turned to some of the people while I am talking it is not as good of an experience for them as it would be to the participant seated right in front of me.

**E (Engage):** After the meet and greet you move into engaging everyone in the group and starting your lecture about whatever topic you have decided on. This portion can include handouts, videos, animal partners and anything really that helps you explain topic. If you go with your own style and not what you think you have to or are supposed to do, you will be more comfortable and your message will touch more people. Personal stories are GREAT during lectures. Especially stories where you can share examples of how you have personally overcome something. Be honest and go deep! The more you can make yourself relatable the more real you will seem to your participants. This will help people to open up to you, to other participants, and as well as help them better retain what it is you are actually teaching.

**E (Exercises):** The exercises are almost always my favorite part of any retreat. There are endless possibilities and you can really use your own creativity here to make your retreat special and your own. This is where people really feel the energy and is truly the soul of the retreat. I like to always have a few different exercises that I offer at each retreat. The reason for this is that everyone learns and experiences things differently. Different types of exercises may be more powerful for different types of people. It can be a lot of fun deciding which exercises to include. A later chapter of this book will cover Reiki Retreat Exercises in more detail. Stay tuned!

**T (Talk):** The talking part of the retreat is really just the discussion or question and answer period at the end. I like to use the word talk because I feel like Reiki Retreat participants offer just as much during this period as I do! Often, they are giving me a new perspective with their point of view or questions! It really is just a talk of people mutually discussing what they shared together in the retreat.

# Chapter 6: Planning Your Retreat Budget

When planning your retreat, it is important to be honest with yourself and have a budget in mind. What are you comfortable spending? Things can really start to add up fast if you allow them to so it is very important to have a number from the beginning that you are comfortable with.

While there is a lot to consider when planning your retreat, the good news is that you do not have to spend a lot of money to have a successful retreat. Depending on where you have it, how many people you have, and how many days your retreat is, can have a big impact on the overall cost. Let's take a look at how much you will need to plan on spending for a basic retreat. The following prices are all calculated with United States Dollars. Please be sure to adjust them for your own location.

**The $200 Retreat:**

$200, how can this be?! Yes, I promise you it can be done! You can have a successful retreat at this price point and it is a great place to start. If your budget is not high you can start with a one day retreat. It will help to have it at your home or the home of a friend so that you do not have to pay a space rent. If this is not possible, outdoor community meeting spaces can sometimes be rented for as low as $50. Churches or other groups that you are a part of might even allow you to use their space for free. Get creative and spend some time researching how much different locations are in your own area.

You can make simple homemade snacks and have a light lunch included in the price of the retreat. You also have the option of not including food and having people buy their own food locally. Drinks should be provided but you can keep it simple by just having water with some sliced up lemon. This should only cost you $5. Coffee and/or tea can be provided for $10. If this is your budget the retreat will need to be limited to a small group of people. Again, this is not a bad thing and can really be a fantastic place to start. Worksheets that are supplied to the class can be emailed to the participants ahead of time. They can print them out and bring them with them or they can look up the information on their phone if they would like to read along while you are going over it during the retreat.

If you want to have a guest speaker it is possible to have one at this price point if you trade services with them or if they are willing to do it for free to get their own business known. Do not be shy. Make phone calls, ask questions and see what your options are. You might be surprised at who would love to speak at your retreat without being financially paid by you.

Any items that are including such as crystals, candles, flowers or herbs should be kept small and simple. Crystals can be purchased for as low as .10cents each, candles for $1.00, flowers for $5 and herb packets for $3. These items can also be provided as take home gifts as well.

Think about using things that you already have. If you are going to buy a few things, try discount stores first. There can be some great finds there that can save you a lot of money. A retreat at this price point will take some creativity but can be done!

**The $500 retreat:**

For the $500 retreat, you can use all of the tips above and extend the time frame to a whole weekend. If you keep the same game plan but extend it an extra day it is completely possible to do it for $500. At this price point you also have the option of sticking to a one day retreat but upgrading the things you are offering during your one day retreat. For example, you can use more materials during your retreat, have a paid guest speaker or even have a package of nice included materials for each participant. These packages can include Reiki jewelry, larger stones and crystals, larger candles, essential oil or whatever else may add value for your topic.

**The $1000 Retreat:**

The $1000 Retreat is a spot where you can really let your creativity start to soar. You are able to do budget friendly week retreats at this price point or more luxurious weekend retreats. To do a week long retreat simply keep the same game plan from the $200 one day retreat. That mode can be replicated throughout the entire week of your retreat. At this price point you are able to rent a retreat space for a weekend at a budget friendly hotel that is very comfortable. You are also able to rent more unique places that offer privacy. Spaces such as condo/ beach houses, cabins, etc. may be rented for your retreat weekend.

If you wish you may get a bit more creative with your meals and other items that you offer. As long as you have the basics in place feel free to do any add-ons that you wish until you reach your budget.

**The $2000 Retreat:**

At this price point you can really have it all. You can rent a nice space and decide where you would like to put different chunks of your money. Perhaps, you would like to have some food catered. You may even be able to work out a discount for this. Perhaps, you would like to put some money towards animal ambassadors, having multiple guest speakers, having high quality Reiki Retreat Kits for all participants, or renting out a special meeting room in a hotel or another special location.

The larger your budget is the more luxurious your retreat can be. However, please remember that no matter what your budget is you can always work out deals. The more deals you work out the more you can have. If you put in the effort you can have a lot of what the $2000 retreat budget offers at the $200 retreat price point. It truly is possible! If you reach a block in what you are doing or what you are wanting, send Reiki to it. I guarantee that if you stay open, a solution will present itself.

When you are trying to decide what your budget is, be sure to remember the importance of what you are charging the participants. If you are doing a simple one day retreat a good place to start is $100-$200 a person. A simple weekend retreat can have you charge $300-$400 per person. The more inclusive retreats or the weeklong retreats can have ticket prices that start at $500+ per person. Be realistic with what you charge and always keep in mind what you yourself would feel comfortable paying for the retreat you are having. Any extra money earned can go back into your retreat business the first few times to give your business a strong financial backbone to stand on.

## *Feeling Guilty About Investing in Your Reiki Retreat?*

Investing in yourself and in your Reiki retreat is not something that you should ever feel guilty about. You must invest both time and money in order to grow and be successful. The more you put into it the better it will be and the more people you will help.

The feeling of guilt is actually a lower vibration and something that you want to send healing energy too. You have to be the best that you can be in order to bring your best self to others. Would you want to go to a practitioner that had a million things going on and Reiki was at the bottom of a long list of tasks they were completing during the day? **Or would you rather go to a practitioner who is calm, cool, collected, and has made Reiki and healing other's a priority in their life?**

**Investing time and money into yourself and your Reiki retreat is not an arrogant or selfish thing to do.** It is, in fact, a form of self-love and a form of love for others as well. Feelings of guilt may pop up from time to time but they can be easily dispelled. How? By Reiki, of course! When this happens to me I immediately send

Reiki to it. Over time it will help alleviate the feelings and will always steer you in the right direction if you are open to it.

**Method to Relieve Healer Guilt:**

1. When you first feel guilty about spending time or money on your retreat, immediately stop whatever you are doing and close your eyes. **Take a short 30 second break.** Sit in that space.
2. Thank yourself for this thought and **make a Power Symbol over yourself**.
3. Say, "**Investing time and money into myself is a sign of self love.** I release any lower energy bringing feelings of guilt with love and acceptance."

4. Next, place your hands cross crossed over your chest (or however you feel comfortable beaming Reiki to yourself) and **send Reiki to yourself for 5min**.
5. At the end of the 5 minutes **give thanks** and move on with your day.

**Remember, you are bringing so much love and healing to the world as a Reiki Practitioner. You have a gift. Never feel guilty!**

# Chapter 7: Expected & Unexpected Issues When Planning a Retreat

As we know, Reiki Retreats are gifts of time that we can give to ourselves to change, heal or grow. It is a time of introspection and releasing everything that does not serve us. As Reiki Practitioners, we are aware of all of this and know what it feels like to grow and heal with the help of energy.

At retreats a lot of energy is exchanged. This is great and means that things are working. However, there may be unexpected things that take place as well that you need to be prepared for as the leader. Below you will find a list of some of the most common expected and unexpected issues that can come up at your retreat. Some of these may never happen or you may experience all of them. In either event, it benefits you to be prepared to have the best retreat possible for all involved. Remember it is not just the attendee learning at the retreat. You as the leader are always learning as well.

**Expected Issues:**

- **Talking:** Depending on who you have sign up you may find that you have a group of highly social people that want to discuss every single thing you cover at great length. While this can add positive energy to your retreat it can also make it hard to stay on schedule. Make sure you know your retreat schedule like the back of your hand. Depending on your retreat location you may not have a lot of flexibility in going over your allotted time frame. When you need to ask people to stop talking make it seem like you are simply redirecting them to speak at another time instead of just silencing them. For example, if people will not stop talking during the question and answer section you could say, *"Wow, I am loving all of the questions* *and the great discussion we are having, We need to move on to our next exercise but I invite all of you to come up and discuss this more with me at our 5pm break. I would love to chat more with all of you. Thank you!"* The more positive and uplifting you make it the more positive and receptive your participants will be.

- **Tardiness:** It is common for at least 1 person to be late for a portion of or all of the starting points of your retreat. This is why I like to plan things at the start of the retreat (meet & greet) and things after the break that are more easily adaptable for people who are running late. If possible, try to just smile at someone who comes in late and let them catch up with what you are doing without you addressing them directly. If you need to verbally guide them to catch up with what you are doing say something like, *"Welcome Chloe! Please join in as much as you can. I will be over to help you catch up in just a few minutes."* It is important to be as inclusive as possible while at the same time not taking anything away from the rest of the group.

- **Weather:** You cannot control everything and that includes the weather! Remember to be flexible and allow for any hiccups the weather may bring.

- **Cold Like Symptoms:** It is extremely common to have people at your retreat with cold like symptoms. These symptoms are usually things like coughing, clearing their throat, runny nose, sore throat, headache, etc. There is a lot of talking going on and sometimes all of the above symptoms can be caused by nerves alone. It is common for people to feel a bit self-conscious at retreats. People are stepping out of their comfort zones and might be a little nervous. I always recommend having water/tea/coffee, tissues, and natural cough drops on hand for participants to feel more comfortable. Soothing oils or calming scents can be beneficial to have as well.

- **Phones:** This is the tech age! It feels like people are on their phones all the time. It can really take away from a retreat when phones are going off and/or people are on them texting constantly. There are two main ways that I recommend for working through this issue. The 1st is to set aside a few minutes at the start of the retreat to discuss phone boundaries. I know it sounds ridiculous but if you don't it most likely will become a problem at some point during your retreat. I always ask people to put their phones on silent or to completely turn them off. I give them a few minutes to do so in case they need to notify anyone that their phone will be off and they will check in with them at a later specific time. This method has always worked for me. The other option is to have a cell phone check in/checkout area upon walking into the retreat. Everyone hands their phone over at the start and it is returned at the end. This method may seem a bit harsh and is not one that I commonly use. Depending on your group it may be something for you to consider using.

**Unexpected Issues:**

- **Physical Cleansing:** Depending on the type of retreat you are having, people may be releasing negative energy during it. This can make people have a physical cleanse and get physically ill! It is not uncommon to have people with cold/flu like symptoms, have to run to the bathroom or even vomit. I have witnessed a whole circle of people vomiting at the same time from releasing negative energy during a sound healing retreat. The instructor had barf buckets for everyone just in case and was prepared. This isn't something meant to scare you but just to show you every possible thing to look out for.

- **Emotional Cleansing:** People may be very emotional at your retreat. They may be having mental breakthroughs, "aha" moments and be releasing a lot of lower energies. This can cause crying, moodiness, highs and lows, outbursts, and apologies. Make sure to remember to keep the bigger picture in mind, that it is a good thing that all lower energies are being released, and most importantly to have a lot of tissues, calming scents and understanding on hand.

- **Asking for a Refund:** Sometimes no matter what you do, or how amazing your retreat is, someone is going to want a refund. It is important to remember to not take it personally and that it is perfectly ok if someone asks for one. Not everyone likes or responds to things the same way. Also, sometimes someone thinks that they are ready to acknowledge and face certain parts of themselves when they sign up. Once faced with the reality and participating in the retreat they might not be able to handle it or have a change of heart. This is ok! Try to remain as calm as possible and remember that everyone is on their own journey with their own timeline. Always, have an upfront refund policy in place that attendees consent to when they sign up. Also, remember that it is ok to be flexible and to go with your gut feeling when someone asks you for a refund.

- **Stage Fright:** Sometimes when we plan a retreat we don't think about how we will feel in the moment talking in front of a group of people. It is normal to feel nervous before hand. There are many techniques you can use if it is hard for you to relax and speak in front of groups of people. Some of these techniques include methods such as looking above everyone's heads when speaking to the group, pretending there is only one person in the room or even pretending that everyone is more uncomfortable than you and showed up in their underwear. If you know ahead of time that you have anxiety when speaking or teaching send some reiki to yourself beforehand so that you know Reiki has your back with staying calm and confident during your retreat. Doing a run through of your retreat ahead of time with friends can be a great confidence builder and can help with speaking anxiety. Another important thing to remember is that often times the participants are just as nervous as you are in the beginning. You have nothing to be ashamed of! Send yourself some Reiki and get out there and lead the retreat.

# Chapter 8: Sending Reiki to Your Retreat

Retreats of any kind take time and energy to plan. There is a lot of hard work and careful planning put into them. With so many different variables coming into play, how do you ensure that the greatest good occurs at the retreat? Is there a way to send positive energy to it? Is there anything that will help make you feel like you can let go? Is there a way to enjoy the retreat you have planned without worrying if you have done everything correctly the whole time? I'm excited to say that there most definitely is!

Reiki can be sent to any situation ahead of time so that the greatest good occurs. It is very easy to do and will help bring you positive energy and peace of mind. In order to send Reiki to your future Reiki Retreat, you only need to follow a few simple steps. It is important to remember to relax and know that Reiki always has your back.

**How to send Reiki to your future Reiki Retreat:**

1. Clear the space you are in like you would with any other Reiki session. This can be done very simply by making a Cho Ku Rei over each wall, ceiling and floor of the space you are in. If you are outside just make the symbol around you as if you are sitting in a cube.

2. Make a large Cho Ku Rei over the center of your body and one over each palm of your hand.

3. Picture your retreat in front of you like you are watching it on a television. Make the distance symbol over it.

4. Set your intention by saying it out loud. It can be as long or as short as you like. For example, you could say something like, "*I am happy that my Reiki Retreat is successful and that the greatest good*

*occurs for all involved. I am happy that I am relaxed, a beacon of light for others and am enjoying every minute of the retreat."*

5. Have your hands face your retreat that you are visualizing is in front of you and beam Reiki to it for 5 minutes. During this time picture that your retreat is as positive and successful as possible.

6. When you are ready to end your session make a backwards Cho Ku Rei over yourself to ground yourself and stop the connection. Give thanks! You are now done.

Sending Reiki to your future retreat is a beautiful thing that you can do to ensure the greatest good occurs for all. You only need to do it once for it to work. Doing it over and over does not provide a different outcome or make your retreat even more successful. You do not want to create a bunch of anxious energy around yourself by not trusting the Reiki process. Allow yourself to trust Reiki and know that it always has your back. The greatest good will always occur with its help. If you have sent Reiki to your retreat ahead of time you can sit back, relax and know that whatever takes place is for the greatest good.

Enjoy your retreat and make it an amazing experience for all involved.

# Chapter 9: Sample Plan Blueprints

## *Sample 1: The 1 Day Retreat*

09:00-09:30am Meet & Greet

09:30-10:30am Lecture #1

10:30-11:30am Exercise Section #1

11:30-12:00pm Questions

12:00-01:00pm Lunch

01:00-01:30pm Meet & Greet after lunch

01:30-02:30pm Lecture #2

02:30-03:30pm Exercise Section #2

03:30-04:00pm Questions

04:00-05:00pm Booth Checkout/One on One Discussions/Networking/Wrap Up

05:00pm Retreat Finished

## *Sample Plan 2: The Weekend Retreat*

Friday night arrivals to retreat location. Have a social hour "check in".

**Saturday (Day 1)**

09:00-09:30am Meet & Greet/ Beverages & Light Breakfast Snacks

09:30-10:00am Pass out the 1<sup>st</sup> day materials. Do a brief overview and a group intention setting 10 minutes meditation for the weekend.

10:00-11:00am Lecture #1

11:00-12:00pm Exercise Section #1

12:00-12:30pm Question & Answer Section

12:30-01:30pm Lunch

01:30-02:00pm Meet & Greet with a 10 minutes group focus meditation on the last ½ of the day.

02:00-03:00pm Lecture #2

03:00-04:00pm Exercise Section #2

04:00-04:30pm Final Question & Answer Section of the day

04:30-05:30pm Extra discussion time, booth viewing, one on one interaction with teacher and/or guest speakers

05:30pm Retreat over for the day

05:30-07:00pm Break

07:00pm-09:00pm Optional Community Dinner

**Sunday (Day 2)**

09:00-09:30am Meet & Greet/ Beverages & Light Breakfast Snacks

09:30-10:00am Pass out the 1st day materials. Do a brief overview and a group intention setting 10 minutes meditation for the day.

10:00-11:00am Lecture #1

11:00-12:00pm Exercise Section #1

12:00-12:30pm Question & Answer Section

12:30-01:30pm Lunch

01:30-02:00pm Meet & Greet with a 10 minutes group focus meditation on the last ½ of the day.

02:00-03:00pm Lecture #2

03:00-04:00pm Exercise Section #2

04:00-04:30pm Final Question & Answer Section

04:30-05:30pm Social hour wrap up, final time to view any booths you have set up, goodbye!

05:30pm Weekend Retreat Finished

Please remember that the samples provided in this book are meant to be a guide. They can and should be individualized by you! Have some fun and make each one your own.

## *A Basic Overall Guide to FOOD VIBRATIONAL LEVELS:*

Food like everything else in the universe has a vibration. Different types of food have different vibrational levels. It's important to pay attention to what your body is trying to tell you and stick to foods of a higher vibrational level. You can Reiki everything you put into your body but the original vibration of what you put in your body remains.

**HIGH VIBRATIONAL LEVEL**

Water, Pure fruit juice, Tea, Fruits, Vegetables, Chicken, Fish, Spices, Jams

If the animal was treated cruelty and was fed hormones or the fruits and vegetables were sprayed with pesticides, then your vibrational level will be lowered.

## MEDIUM VIBRATIONAL LEVEL

Coffee, Other flavored non-alcoholic drinks, Condiments, Bread, Baked goods, Pure butter

## LOW VIBRATIONAL LEVEL

Beef, Pork, Fatty snacks and products, Processed foods, Margarine, Soda, Alcohol

Keep in mind everything in moderation and be sure to still eat things you like. Use this as a guide but be sure to do what you feel is best for you. Only you know what matches your body and vibrational level best! For an added benefit to everything you eat and drink simply draw a Cho Ku Rei over whatever it is you are about to eat/drink.

# Chapter 10: Types of Retreats

You have now selected your retreat location, learned how to plan one and explored some of the sample plans. Next, you are able to decide on what type of retreat you would like to have. Together let's explore the pros and possible cons of different types of retreats. By the end of this chapter you should know exactly what type of retreat is the best fit for you. How exciting! Let's get started!

***1 Day Retreats: The Most Attended!***

One day retreats are a beautiful place to start and usually the most attended. They allow you to offer something at a lower price that is easy to fit into someone's schedule. They are easier to plan and a great stepping stone that allows you to build your Reiki Retreat confidence in.

**Pros:** A great place to start, more affordable, easy to fit into someone's schedule, easily marketable, less pressure, great stepping stone, easy to test out on friends, a great confidence builder

**Cons:** Might not be enough time for you to get all of your information across. You must make the most out of each minute and be sure to carefully follow the timeline.

### *Weekend Retreats: The Most Fun!*

Weekend Retreats can be the most fun and are very worthwhile. They do require a bit more planning than with a one day retreat but as long as your Reiki retreat sample plan blueprint in hand you should be able to accomplish it without a problem! Weekend retreats allow for some unexpected benefits such as time for new friendships to grow. You really have the time to explore every area that you would like to cover and do not have to worry about the 1 day retreat time restraints.

**Pros:** You have more time, mini vacation feel, time for new friendships to form, time to explore your topic, time to excite people and share more of your own experiences, time to include guest speakers.

**Cons:** You must devote more of your own time, will take more of your money up front, you are in teacher mode for the whole weekend.

### Week Long Retreats: The Most Rewarding!

Week long retreats require a lot of patience while planning! Think of it as the same as planning a weekend retreat except with a lot of extras added in. This may seem like too much work to even get started at first but don't let the sound of it stop you from planning. Most week long retreats are not really 7 days long. In my experience they are 4 or 5 days. And even if they are 7 days you have this book to help guide you and make things much easier. Simply use the weekend sample plan provided and add more days following the same schedule. The week long retreat offers the biggest opportunity for growth, breakthroughs and new mindset to form. You can have multiple guest speakers and plan so many different types of activities. Are you a creative person? Planning one may be your dream come true. You will have time to try so many different types of exercises and really have time to talk to all of your participants. There will be ample time for group work and anything that you would like to cover.

**Pros:** Plenty of time for anything you would like to do. You can do it all! Nothing has to be cut out. Multiple guest speakers are possible, friendships can definitely be made, and lifelong breakthroughs can be made.

**Cons:** The greatest amount of upfront costs to you out of all of the retreats. You are "on call" for the whole week. Make sure your friends and family are understanding of this in your personal life and you have care plans for your home life for the week you will be doing the retreat.

# Chapter 11: The Main Topic of Your Retreat

So far in this book you have learned how to plan many different types of basic retreats. Now, all that you need to decide is which topic works best for you! Chances are that you already know exactly what you want to do a Reiki retreat about. If so that is awesome! You can skip right ahead to the next chapter that shows you a topic specific reiki retreat sample plan. If not let's have some fun exploring what Reiki Retreat topic may be best for you.

## *Animal Reiki Retreat*

Animal Reiki Retreats can be so much fun and offer a lot of positive energy to all involved. Do you love animals? Do you want to teach people how to do Animal Reiki or maybe have a community day where Reiki practitioners can get together with their animals? Do you think animals are family and perhaps your animal is treated like your child? Perhaps, you would enjoy teaching how much animal reiki can vary from animal to animal. For example, Equine Reiki can be very different from sending Reiki to a dog. Both are equally special but there are different things to know for each one. If you are an animal person this may be a good topic for you to start your retreat journey on.

## *Confidence Building for Reiki Practitioners Retreat*

Getting a bunch of Reiki Practitioners together to build confidence can be a lot of fun. Everyone already knows the basics of Reiki and what Reiki offers. Here you focus on each person's individual strengths and how to empower themselves. Do you like to make people feel better and watch them gain confidence right before your eyes? This might be the perfect retreat for you to provide for your Reiki community.

### *Reiki Infusion Retreat*

Are you the non-traditional Reiki practitioner? Do you like to explore everything that is Reiki? Do you like to get creative with your practice and find new ways Reiki can help just about any situation? If you like to use Reiki in an assortment of ways this may be the retreat for you to share with others. In this retreat you can teach how Reiki can be combined with almost any other healing modality (even western medicine!) that there is. It offers endless opportunities for fun exercises and appreciation of the limitless possibilities of Reiki.

### *Self-love Reiki Retreat*

Do you love love? Have you seen what a difference self-love can make? Have you witnessed how Reiki can heal any self-love issue? Teaching other's how to combine Reiki self-love with Reiki can be a very powerful experience for all involved. If you are a Reiki Master and see the power of love in all that you do this may be the retreat to put your energy towards. Giving someone the tools of how to love themselves adds loving energy to the world itself. This is a great retreat to lift not only the participants' vibration but the vibration of the entire Earths as well.

### *Living Through Darkness Reiki Retreat*

Have you experienced a dark time in your life that Reiki helped you out of? Have you ever been in the depths of disappear and had an addiction, unhealthy relationship, or were mourning a devastating loss that Reiki brought you out of? This is a great retreat for the sharing of personal stories and to see how powerful of a healing tool that Reiki really is. We learn our greatest lessons while going through dark times, This retreat can teach everyone how Reiki can be a gentle hug for those in despair and how if allowed, can show a lighted path out of the dark to a beautiful new beginning.

### *Cleansing Negative Energy Reiki Retreat*

Have you ever used Reiki to cleanse your house or someone of unwanted dark energy? If you have you know how powerful it is and how amazing it is at getting the job done. This can be a very fun retreat that people get a lot out of. It seems to be the most popular around Halloween and New Years when people seem to be the most aware of spirits and negative energy of all kinds that need to leave their life. If you like to teach others how to clear out bad energy with Reiki this may be the perfect retreat to start out with for you.

## *Bringing Reiki to Children Retreat*

Do you love bringing Reiki to children's lives? Have you noticed what a calming affect it can have on them and how it can teach them how to be empowered and be the creator of peace, harmony, and healing in their own lives? This may be the retreat for you! You can offer it as a retreat where you teach adults how to incorporate Reiki into children's lives. Kids are usually more open minded than adults. Often times, hey will grasp the information faster than adults and might even teach you something in the process! If you love children this retreat can be extremely rewarding.

As you can see the possibilities of main topics for your Reiki Retreat are endless. There are so many fun things that you can share with the Reiki world. If you don't see something in this chapter that speaks to you, please know that you can do a retreat on ANY topic that you like. Perhaps a Reiki retreat on manifesting, renewal, vibration raising, relationship building or letting go is something that calls to you more. If so go with it! The more you love your main topic, the higher the vibration of your retreat will be. Have some fun with your retreat and keep the positive Reiki energy flowing in whichever way you decide to go.

# Chapter 12: Self-love Reiki Retreat Blueprint

The beautiful thing about Reiki Retreats is that they are a gift of time that offer endless possibilities. You can make them as simple or as complex as you like. When planning one I always like to start a with basic plan blueprint. I can then at any time add on to it and experiment with what does and does not work for me. I can even change what worked for me depending on the main topic.

I would like to now share with you a sample plan for a 1 day Reiki Self-love Retreat. Please remember that this is a basic guide that you can and should make your own. Think of it as a blueprint for you to make your own creatively amazing retreat. You can follow this blueprint for any topic you choose. Simply add in your own information related to your topic and topic specific exercises that work for you.

**\*Sample\* 1 Day Self-love Reiki Retreat Blueprint:**

09:00-09:30am Meet & Greet, Set the daily intention, and pass out the self-love items & supplies included in the cost of the retreat.

09:30-10:30am Lecture #1:

- What is self-love?
- What makes us happy and unhappy?
- The Reiki Trash Can
- Love Affirmations
- How can Reiki help?

10:30-11:30am Exercise Section #1

- Journal exercise in self-love – what makes us happy and unhappy

- Reiki Trash Can Practice Game
- Affirmation creation, practice and infusion with Reiki

11:30-12:00pm Questions

12:00-01:00pm Lunch

01:00-01:30pm Guided Self-love Meditation with Reiki Infusion

01:30-02:30pm Lecture #2

- Importance of self-reiki for self-love
- Self-love Meditation Lesson
- Color Therapy with Reiki
- Love Crystals with Reiki

02:30-03:30pm Exercise Section #2

- Self-Reiki for self-love practice
- Self-love meditation practice
- Color work practice with reiki
- Crystal work practice with reiki

03:30-04:0pm Questions

04:00-05:00pm Participants are invited to check out the tables you have set up offering self-love items, one on one discussions, networking, goodbye!

05:00pm Retreat Finished

## Basic Exercise to work on Self-Love with Reiki

Creating self-love is one of the best things you can do for yourself. Once you have added it to your life, it will help you change anything else you feel needs to be balanced as well. After all, the healthier you are and the more full of love you are, the more you can help others.

**Self-love Reiki Exercise:**

1. Sit in a comfortable, **relaxing space**, similar to one where you would do a meditation. If nature or relaxing music helps your body to relax than put some on before the start of the session.

2. Lay down on the ground and allow yourself to **just slowly breathe for a few minutes**.
3. At this time make **one large power or master symbol** and then make an **emotional healing symbol** as well.
4. Lay in this space and allow yourself to relax. **Visualize** that an angel or pure healer from another realm is standing in front of you dressed in flowing, radiant, white clothing. They hold a crystal clear glass pitcher filled with loving pink light. They have come with this pitcher to help you heal and bring self-love into your life. They stand over you with the pitcher and gently pour the pink light over you. It feels like refreshing water nourishing every ounce of your being that it touches. Notice how your body feels as the light pours over you from your head to your toes. Let yourself be cleansed and healed by this light for about 5 minutes. After 5 minutes the angel/healer leaves your side.
5. At this time, **picture** something about yourself that you don't like. Visualize that this issue comes out of the core of your body and hovers directly above you. Visualize that a pink ball of light encircles this issue and covers it in love. Make a an emotional healing

symbol over this bubble and let it stay there for about 2 minutes. Beam Reiki to it with your eyes or hands as you continue to stay in your meditative space. The light becomes so strong that it bursts this issue into a thousand pieces. It is no longer in your life. It has moved on and so have you.

6. **Allow** any negative thoughts about yourself to come up to the surface and do this same exercise for each one. If there are too many issues for you to do in one session simply do a few sessions throughout the week until you have covered everything that has come up. Once done with your session make one large power or master symbol over yourself.

7. **Thank Reiki and the healing power of Love for the healing they brought you. You are now on your journey to a beautiful place full of self-love.**

# Chapter 13: Items to Sell at a Reiki Retreat

Reiki retreats offer a great venue to sell Reiki related items. I recommend having a table set up at the retreat devoted to things that you are handing out as well as having a separate table that is devoted to things that you are offering the participants of the retreat to buy. For instance, if you are having a self-love retreat here is an example of things people can view at each table.

## *Self-love Retreat Item Tables:*

**Table #1: Sample Items *Included* in the Price of the Retreat**

- Self-love Reiki Box – rose quartz, self-love affirmations, guided self-love meditation, candle, self-love Reiki infused bracelet
- Class handouts – key points, sample plans, visuals, contact info, etc…
- Any class materials that you are providing that are specific to that day of the retreat

**Table #2: *Extra* Items that Are Available to Purchase**

- Other possible crystals that can add to self-love work besides rose quartz
- Other Reiki infused jewelry besides what is included in the class
- Special Discounted classes and Reiki session information that you offer to only Reiki retreat participants
- Discounted offer information for the participants from any guest speaker
- Any other extra that is related but not included in the retreat

Having items that are included in the retreat as well as those that people can purchase if they wish creates a nice balance. That way people feel like they are already being given some cool stuff and that the retreat is not just a store front for people trying to sell their products. Your included items should have everything that your participant needs for the retreat. It should make them feel special and set your retreat apart from others. If they love what is included and feel like you are more focused on teaching them at the retreat than focused on selling them products, they will be more interested in what is at your for sale table. The table with the "extras" will be seen as a fun place to check out and they will be curious about it rather than be put off by it.

**Great items to include at any Reiki retreat:**

- Reiki infused jewelry
- Crystals/stones infused with Reiki
- Guided Meditations that can be used with Reiki
- Spiritual Music
- Reiki infused candles
- Class Handouts
- Special Discounted offers that relate to the retreat or a pamphlet with other classes, retreats and services that

you or other guest speakers are offering the participants
- Coffee/tea/water
- Light snacks
- Recommendations for other classes of benefit

The tables at your retreat are a great place for people to gather during breaks as well as at the end of the retreat to network and/or ask questions. The tables should be unique to you and what retreat topic you are doing.

## *Crystals & Chakras & Reiki:*
## *A Basic Guide*

 Root Chakra:

Tiger's Eye, Hematite, Bloodstone, Garnet, Ruby, Red/Lodestone

 Sacral Chakra:

Smoky Quartz, Orange stones, Carnelian, Red Jasper

 Solar Plexus:

Moonstone, Yellow/Amber, Topaz, Argonite, Malachite

 Heart Chakra:

Rose Quartz, Green/Emerald, Tourmaline, Pink Calcite

 Throat Chakra:

Blue Lace Agate, Celestite, Aquamarine, Blue/Turquoise

 Third Eye Chakra:

Quartz, Indigo/Lapis, Lazuli, Sodalite

 Crown Chakra:

Violet/Amethyst, Clear Quartz, Clear Calcite, Diamond, Ametrine

## Reiki crystal cleansing methods:

1. Make the Master symbol (or whatever symbol you feel guided to use) over each crystal. Then make the same symbol on the palm of your hand and hold the crystal with your hand closed around it for 5 minutes. During this time, imagine that Reiki is cleansing anything negative from the crystal that was picked up before/after using it.

2. Take a bowl of saltwater, add the crystals to it and then make the Master symbol (or whatever symbol you are called to use) over it. Reiki the bowl of water for 5 minutes and then let the crystals sit in the bowl of water for about another 20 minutes.

# Chapter 14: Guest Speakers

Guest speakers can add an abundance of positivity to your retreat and offer a wealth of information. Ideally, the guest speaker should be someone who is an expert in a specific area that relates to your retreat, or has a personal story that relates to your retreat, or is a great teacher that can add a lot of extra value to your retreat.

If you are doing a 1 day retreat you might not decide to include a guest speaker. If you are doing a weekend or week long retreat you may decide that having different people speaking is something that you would like to offer to your participants. You will have time with the longer retreats to expand on your topic and offer more information to your participants. As an example, for a self-love retreat you may want to include a guest speaker who has a powerful real life story of finding their own self-love. Perhaps, you would like to include a speaker who specializes in meditation who can lead the group in a special self-love guided meditation. Perhaps, you have decided to do your retreat on cleansing with Reiki. If that is the case you may want to have a guest speaker who has a lot of experience with cleansing spaces or perhaps a mental health expert who can discuss the mental health aspects of hoarding and what huge benefits physically clearing a space can have.

The possibilities of guest speakers are endless. They do not have to be a Reiki practitioner but they should be someone who has a lot to offer to make your retreat special. You may be thinking that you would like to have a guest speaker but that having one would be very costly. Take a chance and reach out to a few different people that you are interested in having speak at your retreat. You may be able to trade services with them instead of paying them money. Sometimes people will teach or speak to a group as a community outreach type thing or a way to give back. They may also be interested in speaking for free if they have an interest in being a student for the remainder of the retreat or if they feel speaking will give their own business some positive exposure.

Make sure that you give the guest speaker an allotted amount of time so that they can plan a meaningful talk with your group that is within the time frame you have set up. Remember, that it is your retreat and that you are the leader. You should set up all time guidelines, ask them for an outline of their presentation and know what they are going to present to your participants ahead of time. A good way to go about this is to have a meeting with them ahead of time where they give you an example of what they are going to talk about. You can also ask any questions that you might have and together come up with a positive lesson for the participants. The guest speaker is offering something at your event. It is important to remember that your name is on the line and that you are sure that you are 100% comfortable and supportive of everything that they will be contributing to your retreat.

Collaboration can make your retreat even more amazing. Just make sure that you are aware of what will be happening during the guest speaker's time and be sure to as always plan ahead.

# Chapter 15: Animal Partners

Animal Partners can offer some amazing benefits to any retreat. They can help in teaching different things, help people relax, can help break the ice and make everything a lot more fun.

If you are hosting a retreat at a home or at another location with animals make sure that your participants are aware when they sign up. While I personally love animals and find them very relaxing this is not true of everyone. It is their right to know what they are signing up for. Some people have severe allergies or fear when it comes to animals. A beloved cat who is cheerfully greeting members of your retreat may not seem like a negative thing to you. However, if one of your participants has a cat allergy or some other issue that prevents them from being at a retreat with animals that is a big deal to them. If they don't know that there will be animals present ahead of time this miscommunication on your part can cause what would have been a positive retreat experience into a bad one before the retreat even started. Be sure that everyone knows exactly what they are signing up for. You can do a short, one line statement on the sign-up page saying, *We have loving animal ambassadors at our retreats. Please let us know at the time of sign up if you have an animal allergy or other animal issue that prevents you from participating in our retreat.* Something like this can go a long way in keeping communication open about just who may be hanging out at your special retreat. I find that animals offer extra blessings at retreats and love to have them around whenever possible. If you are an animal person I highly recommend having them at yours.

When I was learning how to love myself again, I did a lot of work with horses. So it is no wonder that the more I got into Reiki the more I got into Equine Reiki as well. Equine Reiki and Animal Reiki of all kinds can be a great thing to add into a weekend long or week long retreat.

Animals are selfless and are great at showing us how to love. You know what else they are a natural at? They are able to sense negative energy of any kind! They are great to include in any retreat that works with Reiki and cleansing negativity.

When you have animals at a retreat location, please try to remember that you need to look at the business side of things. This means that you MUST do things like check insurance policies and make sure that you are covered in all areas. Also, remember to think of what is healthy and comfortable for the animals. Do not stress the animal out under any conditions! If you are wanting, to show people how beneficial Equine Reiki is then it is important to know what the horse is comfortable with and not comfortable with ahead of time. Does the horse enjoy being around new people? Does it scare easily? Is it ok with laughter or sudden sounds that it might not be expecting? Does it like to be a leader? Is the horse head strong or easy going? Does it have experience in a therapeutic setting with people?

You as the leader of the retreat should never under any circumstance have an animal be a part of your retreat that you have not met before. This is not good or fair for the animal or for you! The animal should be a being that you know and whose energy you are in tune with. They should enjoy people and enjoy being a part of the group. No matter what good intentions there are if an animal is uncomfortable it is an abusive situation and not one of positivity.

If you plan ahead and take proper precautions, Animal Partners during Reiki Retreats can offer an amazing experience that leaves the participants with life long memories. If you are an animal lover I highly recommend taking the time to carefully plan some positive animal interaction time at your retreat.

# Chapter 16: Protecting Yourself Before Group Exercises & Energy Exchange

During Reiki energy is exchanged, it is *extremely* important to protect yourself before Reiki group exercises or energy exchange of any kind. If you are an Empath, it is even easier to pick up other's energy. You do not want to be picking up things that are not yours. This can lead to all kinds of complications or unwanted problems during group exercises. You want to put your energy together to raise the vibration of a space or to practice something individually and then report your experience to the group, so that everyone can learn. You do *not* want to be passing negative or fearful energy mistakenly from person to person. The good news is that if you simply protect yourself with Reiki at the start of the retreat, you won't have to worry about any negative energy exchange during the retreat.

I like to lead an exercise at the start of every retreat that teaches you how to shield yourself for the day. It takes under 5 minutes to do and is something that I do every day regardless of what my plans are. I like to call it the Reiki Protection Bubble but I have also heard it called the Reiki shield and even a spiritual condom. No matter what you like to call it, it works and gets the job done!

### The Reiki Protection Bubble

1. Make a Cho Ku Rei symbol over yourself.
2. Visualize a big ball of white light surrounding you.
3. Say out loud or to yourself quietly, *"I encircle myself in the white light of God's love and divine protection. All negative things must leave now!"* You may easily change this statement to match any of your own personal beliefs. That's it! You are protected.

If at any time through the retreat or your day you feel like something is bothering you or the energy is bad, go ahead and do this process to yourself at any time. It is a great "pick me up" and keeps your vibration up knowing that you are protected. It also keeps things away from you. Negativity of all kinds (including people) are repulsed by you and do not even know why!

Now that we know how to protect our own energy zone, let's move to the next chapter and explore how much fun we can have with group exercises!

## Reiki Salt Space Cleanse Method

**1. Prepare for space cleanse**: Purchase enough salt to cleanse your entire space. I used whatever was on sale at the store. I know some people will only buy pure sea salt when cleansing. I believe that any salt will work. Do what speaks to you. You will need enough to put a small amount in each corner of your space as well as sprinkling though out. Also, be sure to get enough small glasses out to use in each of the main corners of the space. I do not recommend using plastic. If you do not have enough glasses then pouring some directly on the floor is ok.

**2. Stand in the middle of the space and picture a white light encircling it.** Say to yourself or out loud, *"I surround this space in the white light of God's love and* *divine protection."* Substitute whatever your own views are with this statement. Saying what you believe has the most power. For example, you could use the word higher power or source instead of the word God. Then, make a power or master symbol in front of you in the middle of the space while asking Reiki for the greatest good to occur in this cleansing.

**3. Pour salt** (I usually use a few tablespoons for each corner) **into the glasses you are going to use.** Make a power symbol or master symbol over each glass and say, *"Only peace, love, and understanding is allowed in thisspace. No negativity or negative people may cross into this space."* Place each glass you have prepared into the farthest corners of the space.

4. Next, **pour a solid line of salt across the main entrances.** I did this at the front door, back door, and garage door. I also did it at the main sliding doors and windows that I like to have open. After you have poured your line of salt make a power or master symbol over it and say the same thing as before, *"Only, peace, love, and understanding is allowed in this space. No negativity or negative people may cross into this space."*

5. Finally, **walk around your space and sprinkle salt** anywhere that you feel you might need a little extra positivity and make a power or master symbol over it.

**6. Give thanks and change the salt once a week for 4 weeks.** Dispose of the salt in your trash can. If you poured your salt directly onto the floor then simply vacuum it up and then toss in the trash can. After that use this method whenever you feel called to do so.

# Chapter 17: Fun Group Exercises

Group exercises can really help to set the tone of your retreat and leave lasting memories for all involved. They can create a sense of community and can help create several breakthrough moments. Applying Reiki to group settings can make you feel how universal Reiki is and may help the participant to be able to relate to the energy deeper. There is a special power in group work that can really help to change vibration frequencies right before your eyes. There are so many different types of exercises and really just about anything can be infused with Reiki. I have tried to provide an assortment of different examples for you here but please remember you can come up with your own exercises! Use one or two of the exercises below or simply read through all of them and let them spark ideas in you of your own unique exercises.

### Reiki Plant Vibration Exercise

This is a great exercise to do together during a week-long retreat. You should have a few different plants on hand that look like they are not doing well. Take a picture of each plant at the start of the retreat before any Reiki energy is sent to it. At the start of the exercise, break the participants into small groups to beam Reiki to a plant for 10 minutes.

This process should be repeated for 10 minutes each day of the retreat. There should also be one plant that the entire group beams Reiki to at the same time for 10 minutes.

The last day of the retreat have a table set up with the before picture of each plant next to what each plant now looks like. There should be visual evidence of what the group Reiki energy was able to accomplish during the time of the retreat. This is a great tangible lesson of what group Reiki is able to accomplish.

## The Power of Your Hands Exercise

This exercise doesn't take up much time and is great at helping people to gain confidence in the fact that Reiki really can be felt coming through their hands.

Have the participants break up into small groups of 3-8 people depending on the size of your overall retreat group. Have each of the small groups sit together in a circle.

Next, have each person make a Cho Ku Rei symbol over each one of their own palms of their hands.

Next, have them hold their own hands together (palm to palm) in a prayer like position for 1 minute asking that Reiki charge their own personal space. Next, have them place one had out to each side of them. Their left palm should be touching the palm of the person to their left while their right palm should be touching the palm of the person to their right. Everyone in the circle should have their palms connected. Have everyone stay in this connected space for 2 minutes.

At the end of the 2 minutes have everyone discuss what they felt and if they could feel the Reiki energy coming from the people next to them. The most common answer received is yes!

### Self-love Expansion Exercise

This exercise requires that you share a bit about yourself but the pay-off is huge.

Everyone will be put in groups of 3 people. This allows for small sessions but you still get the feel of a group. Everyone will have a sheet of paper where they write down one thing that they don't like about themselves. You also write down a list of things you would like to feel about yourself.

Next, each person will write down something nice that they have noticed about the person or people next to them. When everyone is done you will take turns sharing what you don't like about yourself and something nice that each of you notices about each other immediately. At the end you will burn the small piece of paper with your dislike comment on it to release it to be healed.

This exercise shows you how much your own mind plays in self-love. Other people are able to immediately see positive things about you. What do you need to work on so that you can see these same things?

## Reiki Cleanse Exercise

This is a fun exercise that can be done in a weekend or week long Reiki cleansing retreat.

Pick a location that you would like to practice group cleansing at. It can be a separate house, campground, hotel or office building that the retreat is at. Pick a few areas ahead of time that you would like to have the group practice cleansing with Reiki. This exercise should be completed at the end of the retreat once everyone has learned the tips they need to successfully complete the exercise together.

At the start of the exercise have everyone do a walk-through of all the spaces that are to be cleared together. Have everyone take a journal (or phone along) where they can write or type what they feel in each room.

After the walkthrough has been complete break people up into small groups. Assign each group to a different area of the location to cleanse. They should spend no more than 10 minutes clearing the space. At the end of the 10 minutes have everyone meet back up.

You will then do a walk through together of all the spaces that were cleared. Have everyone again write or type everything that they notice about the space now.

After everyone is done go back to your main group meeting spot and discuss the findings. The spaces should be much lighter and everyone will build confidence in the improvement they have seen in all of the spaces that were cleansed.

**Intuition Building Exercise**

This exercise can be done in groups of 2 or 3 and is so much fun to try out. It really lets you experiment with Reiki and see what you can do with the different Reiki signs.

Have the 1st person sit in front of the person they are going to try to intuitively communicate with. Have them make 1 Cho Ku Rei, 1 Sei Hei Ki and 1 Hon Sha Ze Sho Nen over the forehead (3rd eye) of the person they will be communicating with.

Next have the person sit in front of them and recite one short sentence in their head that they wish to communicate with them over 2 minutes. It should be something short and simple. Something like, "Your hair is beautiful, I love animals, my favorite color is blue, what is your favorite country?" Whatever it is make sure that is the only thing that is repeated for 2 minutes.

At the end of the exercise have them ask the person what message they think was being sent to them. Have everyone write down the results on a piece of paper. After they answer, keep this exercise going so that each person in the group can have a turn sending and receiving distance messages with Reiki.

The more you do this exercise the more accurate you will find that you are.

**The Human Mirror Exercise**

This exercise is great for participant bonding and shows us the power and uniqueness of each individual.

The eyes are truly the doorway to the soul and this exercise will leave you feeling compassion and love for people that only a few days before were complete strangers. To start have several groups of 2 chairs setup facing each other. There should be enough for each person to have a partner. Next, each person will take a seat and silently face the person in front of them. You will sit silently for 20 minutes. During this time there will be no speaking. You are however encouraged to try to send energy to the person through your eyes.

At the end of the exercise everyone will have 5 minutes to write down what they experienced in their retreat journal.

This exercise can be very intense and a lot can be learned in a short 20 minutes!

**Group Fluidity Exercise**

This exercise can show your participants how powerful energy can be and how it can be felt without having your eyes open.

Have the participants in the group get in a large circle. Have everyone close their eyes and send energy to the person in front of them while receiving energy from the person behind them. The point is to try and move your hands in the same way you feel the person sending you energy is moving theirs. No physical touching is allowed.

After 10-15 minutes ask everyone to open their eyes. The result should be that everyone's hands are unexpectedly positioned in exactly the same way.

It should be a unique and fun experience that teaches the group the true power of energy.

# Chapter 18: Reiki Take Home Gifts...Thank you!

Now that you have learned all of the basics of planning any type of retreat, I'd like to spend a short moment discussing what a big impact a small little Reiki take home gift can have. Your participants have given you a piece of their lives to help them grow and learn something new. They have trusted you and thought that you had something really special that you could offer them. This is the time to show them how grateful you are and how special they are to you as well. It also ends the retreat on a positive note and will hopefully bring them joy and a reminder of how much fun they had at your retreat whenever they look at the Reiki take home gift that you gave them.

*Spreading Joy with Reiki Gifts*

Having something tangible to take home from Reiki retreats seems to really help a lot of people to move forward on their personal healing or spiritual journey. There are a few different ways that I have done this and I have found all to work great. Try each one out and see which method resonates best with you.

**How to Infuse Small Gifts with Reiki:**

**1. Reiki Box Method**

Places a bundle of stones, small candles or whatever other small gifts you wish to infuse with Reiki energy in a special Reiki box. This Reiki box does not need to be anything special. It can be anything from a cardboard box to a hand carved wooden one. Use what you have. Reiki does not discriminate. Make a large Master or Power symbol over the box and then send Reiki to it for 5 minutes. I like to always set the intention that the Reiki energy help bring love and the best healing energy possible to the recipient of each piece. You may then either leave the Reiki infused objects in the box until you give them away or you may take them out and put them in a safe place.

Before handing a piece out to someone I scan my hand over the box and see which piece causes a vibration on my hand. That is my sign of which piece to give them.

**2. Infusion Bubble Method**

Place all of the objects you'd like to infuse with Reiki on a table in front of you. Visualize a bubble of love and positive energy slowly surrounding the group of objects. Beam Reiki to this bubble for 5 minutes. Make a grounding symbol at the end to stop the stream of Reiki flowing to the objects. Your gifts are now infused with Reiki.

### 3. Reiki Hand Infusion

If you feel called to give someone an object that has not already been infused with Reiki there is a very fast and easy method you can use simply by holding the object in your hand. Make a Master or Power symbol on the palm of your hand. Pick up the object and hold it in the palm of your hand. Visualize Reiki flowing from the palm of your hand directly into the object. Once you are done beaming Reiki to it make a grounding symbol over the object with your other hand to end the flow of Reiki. Hand the object directly to the person you wish to give it to.

**Giving small unexpected Reiki infused gifts to people is such an easy way to spread joy and positive energy.** **Often times the act of giving a small unexpected gift will immediately send waves of joy, love and happiness out into the Universe.**

The Reiki take home gifts that I enjoy giving are not anything big or extravagant. They should just be something small and unexpected that was not listed as an included item when they signed up. I like to gift everyone with a reiki infused bracelet, stone or candle that shares healing properties with whatever main topic the Reiki Retreat was covering. This way they have a token of positivity from me to them and they know that I really care about them and the topic of the Reiki Retreat.

Thank you for entrusting me with your time to learn about creating your very own Reiki retreat. You now have all the tools to go out and gift people with what you have to offer. Reiki retreats are gifts of time that can change a person's whole life. They lead to healing in unexpected ways and keep the power of Reiki healing going strong. Get creative, have some fun and with this guide go out and fearlessly start your very own Reiki Retreat journey!

# About the Author

Justine Melton is a Reiki Master Teacher, Psychic Medium & Intuitive Counselor. She loves to teach people how to embrace their own power and to live their best life possible. She believes that Reiki and self-love can create miracles in your life and that you are never too old to have the life you want. She is passionate about teaching, writing and mentoring in the Reiki field. She has used Reiki in her own life to heal, manifest and change in all areas. She loves to share this energy now with others.

Justine is a regular contributor at Reiki Rays and can be found at <u>SerenityOfTheMindAndSoul.com</u>.

Made in the USA
Columbia, SC
12 June 2019